T0207688

A
WAY
IN
YOUR
DESERT

BARIBUTSA M., JACQUELINE

authorHOUSE

AuthorHouse™
1663 Liberty Drive
Bloomington, IN 47403
www.authorhouse.com
Phone: 1 (800) 839-8640

Published by AuthorHouse 11/08/2019

ISBN: 978-1-7283-3536-0 (sc)
ISBN: 978-1-7283-3537-7 (hc)
ISBN: 978-1-7283-3535-3 (e)

".....I will even make a way in the wilderness and the rivers in the desert."-**Isaiah 43:19**

CONTENTS

DEDICATION

I dedicate this book to my father Baributsa Se Gaju Ladislas for giving me a name. I inherited from him love for people, commitment to deep things of God, meditation on the word of God and consistent prayer.

To my mother Therese Ruseka Nyirabashyitsi who passed away last year, for being my model and mentor; and the one who taught me by her many examples courage, ambitions, and responsibility as a mother. She gave me her sense of achievement as business woman, love of good work and excellence.

I also dedicate this first book to my children who are my first support in my work and achievements since their childhood. Guy-Andre Pierlot my eldest who is my partner in the Ministry and my Editor and Translator. Roland Pierlot my second son who is my advisor and business manager in Europe. Thanking him also for his support in our first church, Bary's Ministries Grâce sur Grâce in Belgium.

To my sisters Domina, Dona and Colette Baributsa for being my intercessors, my support, and my advisors, I say "Thank you so much for all your work in my life. I am grateful to you. My God will reward all of you in Jesus name."

ACKNOWLEDGMENT

I wish to acknowledge Bishop Martin Lukanda Mutyebele who passed away recently, for recognizing and ordaining me as pioneer woman pastor empowered to plant a church.

I also acknowledge Philippe Pierlot, the father of my children, for your tremendous supports in the running of Bary's Ministries in both Rwanda and in Belgium.

I wish to appreciate Lauren Saba Childs, Artist, Creative Director and Owner of Fort Works Art, for being so good to me, encouraging and believing in me that I could achieve success in this country.

And to all members of Bary's Ministries Grâce sur Grâce Namur (Belgium) and Pastor Lucie Ntumba Kabangu; I say "Thank You" for your faithfulness and great work you have been doing since I relocated to the United States of America (USA).

Thank you Pastor Jean Ntihi my brother in law, for being always there to support me when it's needed. Also for all your prayers and counsels to me and my children. My life was touched by you a lot in many different ways. May God bless you all!

FOREWORD

The difficulties you face in your desert experience give you an opportunity to discover yourself, to give birth to new projects, fresh ideas, different perspectives and renewed goals.

It is a season of self-reflection and reconstruction. Don't consider what's old. Your future is ahead, waiting for you. Go for it!

Between Egypt and the Promised
Land, there was a desert.
If you want to reach your destiny,
You must accept your desert.

INTRODUCTION

What comes to your mind when you hear the word "Desert"? What are your first words to describe it? Drought, sand, thirst, arid and infertile land, hunger, fatigue, burning heat, misery, poverty, hardship, despair, death...etc?

So many words and emotions immediately come to mind to define this very special place. However, I would like to tell you that beyond the wonder and fears it can arouse, the desert also offers a lot of:

- Graces
- Blessings
- Opportunities for you to make a breakthrough in your life and discover where your real potential lies.

During my journey in the desert of Air in the Sahara, I saw things that still astonish me today. There we had the privilege of visiting Mr. Soulé's plantation. The sight of all his plants, fruit trees and vegetables in the middle of a land yet so hostile was amazing. They are all so different from everything we knew in terms of their shape, taste and size-a real pleasure for our eyes as well as for our palates.

One day Mr. Soulé offered me a lemon from his garden and let me pick a few sheaves of wheat, which I brought back to Belgium to edify the members of *Grace upon Grace*, the church I founded several years ago. This lemon was the size of a melon whose color resembled that of a beautiful yellow sun. As for the wheat fields, they reminded me of the one mentioned in Matthew 13:24-30 where Jesus talks about sorting the wheat from the chaff. We also saw water springs, wells, villages and the wonderful people who live there. There are keys that you will need to acquire at any cost if you want to pass through any desert. These are:

- Faith
- Hope
- Patience
- Endurance
- Courage
- Action
- The ability to proclaim positive words and minimize negative language

The Bible unequivocally states that God is omniscient (He knows everything), omnipotent (He can do anything) and omnipresent (He is everywhere). We can then count on Him to visit us in any kind of desert that we are passing through, to plant oases, and to bring us rest as long as we trust Him and wait for His divine intervention with faith and perseverance.

CHAPTER ONE

TRUST AND WAIT

This is not synonymous with crossing your arms and staying passive. Quite the opposite! Going through a difficult time while remaining inactive is the perfect recipe for depression, which will eventually lead to potential destruction. In Isaiah 49: 14-15 we read:

> *"But Zion said, 'The LORD has forsaken me, the Lord has forgotten me.'*
>
> *Can a mother forget the baby at her breast and have no compassion on the child she has borne?*
>
> *Though she may forget, I will not forget you!"*

God Himself in the above passage tells us that He will never abandon us! Therefore, pray, fast and meditate. Serve Him and He will act *in His time* and *in His own way*.

Be Vigilant and Stay Active

It is imperative for you to be alert when everything goes wrong. Pay attention to the new habits that accompany emerging difficulties or the growing desert experience of your life. Sort it out and get rid of the behaviors that appear in the tragic circumstances surrounding you.

Make sure that your mind is busy with various tasks and prevent it from focusing solely on your problems. This could take over all your attention and dangerously affect your morale, health and social life. Therefore, in order to shift your attention away from your problems and over-come, I encourage you to do some of the activities listed below:

- Walking
- Swimming
- Jogging
- Reading
- Writing
- Gardening
- Home improvement
- Sewing
- Cleaning of your home
- Going to movies
- Taking classes

- Praying
- Volunteering service
- Making yourself available and useful to others

Loneliness and isolation will get you very quickly sucked into a depression. Avoid them at all cost.

You may wonder whether these would work. Of course, they would. I've applied these principles in my personal life. In addition, I decided to develop other activities, some of which are completely new to me like creating cosmetic products by inspiration and gardening of flowers and vegetables in my home etc.

I even created my own cooking recipes for which I resolved to teach and release a book very soon. I did it for my own self development but also to help, at my humble level, people who struggle to indulge themselves with healthy, simple and inexpensive dishes. I also want these recipe classes to be accessible to all categories of men, women, girls and boys, even teenagers.

The season of your desert or difficulties is the right time for you to dig deeper into yourself and discover talents, desires, projects, ambitions and skills that were buried, undiscovered and therefore unexplored. In other words, the difficulties we pass through can become an opportunity to discover our potentials and thereby be fulfilled as a person. However, lessons must be learned from these discoveries, and immediate actions taken to turn them into something productive. These are to:

- evolve on a personal level
- benefit your society, church, neighborhood or your direct environment.

Going back to my culinary ambitions, the idea of teaching cooking classes came to me in November 2015. I had a strong feeling that it would open doors for me on the job market. The spirit of God speaks sometimes in one way, sometimes in another. He places in us a deep conviction of what He is about to do for us, in us and through us. Back then, I shared what I received from the Lord with my children and some of my family members, having concretized it into a feasible plan but I didn't know if they believed me or not. However, one of my nephews strongly advised me against it, telling me it would not work because of platforms like YouTube where knowledge is already freely shared worldwide.

Sometime later, my son's friend from Belgium visited us and I shared with him my idea. His enthusiasm and the way he appreciated the dishes I made for him greatly encouraged me.

Six days later, I started a new job based on my skills as a cook and in addition to my work as an educator.

After two years of absolute desert experience through the job market since October 2013, my life finally changed completely.

My advice to you is to endeavor to cultivate a serious, deep and sincere relationship with the Holy Ghost through meditation and prayer, and you will be amazed how God can guide and strengthen you when you pray.

CHAPTER TWO

UNDERSTANDING THE IMPORTANCE OF WAITING

Waiting means being patient or show patience. The latter is one of the fruits of the Spirit mentioned in the fifth chapter of the epistle to the Galatians. There are two things that are extremely difficult to possess when problems strike you from all sides: faith and patience.

Your faith – or your trust in God – severely diminishes when you are not well. The biblical account of these characters we classify as "Heroes of Christian faith" show that this phenomenon indiscriminately affects everyone. But how do we explain this?

In reality, lack of faith appears when we are unable to imagine a rational and adaptable solution to our problems. Therefore, we conclude that God will not be able to solve it either. We begin to make mechanical prayers for which we do not believe that God will answer.

If you find yourself in what I am describing, I would like to encourage you or at least remind you that we have an OMNIPOTENT God who is a very present help in the time of trouble! His almighty power defies centuries of afflictions, distances, laws, curses and failures. Stop panicking and know that He is God!

Patience is a delicious fruit when you know how to savor it, and it encompasses many other qualities. Assurance would certainly be at the top of the list. Assurance is the belief that sooner or later everything will be alright if you are patient enough while waiting for your solution, answer, deliverance or blessing. It is the Holy Ghost who inscribes in the depths of your soul that the Lord will act *in His own time* and *for His own glory.*

During the time of waiting, do not curse but bless. Do not lament but confess that the Eternal God will never abandon you. Do not hurt anyone, and move away from the very people who may be the source of your problems. Do not also be jealous or envious of the success and happiness of others. God NEVER forgets His own! Isaiah 49:8-11, 14-16:

⁸This is what the LORD says: "In the time of my favor I will answer you, and in the day of salvation I will help you; I will keep you and will make you to be a covenant for the people, to restore the land and to reassign its desolate inheritances,

⁹ to say to the captives, 'Come out,' and to those in darkness, 'Be free!' "They will feed beside the roads and find pasture on every barren hill. ¹⁰ They will neither hunger nor thirst, nor will the desert heat or the sun beat down on them. He who has compassion on them will guide them and lead them beside springs of water.

¹¹ I will turn all my mountains into roads, and my highways will be raised up.

¹⁴ But Zion said, "The LORD has forsaken me, the Lord has forgotten me."

¹⁵ "Can a mother forget the baby at her breast and have no compassion on the child she has borne? Though she may forget, I will not forget you!

¹⁶ See, I have engraved you on the palms of my hands; your walls are ever before me."

In Isaiah 46:4, The Lord declares: ***"Even to your old age and gray hairs I am he, I am he who will sustain you. I have made you and I will carry you; I will sustain you and I will rescue you."***

Prayer

Amen! Thank you Lord, for your Word. We take every promise you said to make them ours, in the name of Jesus. Help us to keep your commandments and honor you in everything we do, say and think. So that we may experience what you say in your Word: ***"If only you had paid attention to my commands, your peace would have been like a river, your well-being like the waves of the sea."***

(Isaiah 48:18)

A song comes to my mind, may it encourage you:

Faithful God, you never change
Eternal, my rock, my peace
Powerful God I lean on you
And I cry to you because you're my God
I need you
You are my rock on the day of distress
And if I fall, you lift me up

In the storm your love brings me back to the shore
You are my only hope Lord.

First day at the Taylors

It was my first day at work. I arrived at 9:30 a.m. and waited until 10 a.m. when I was supposed to start. I told the man at the entrance of the gated community that I was ahead of schedule and that I wanted to make sure I arrived on time. He smiled and told me that it's better to arrive early than late. Indeed a piece of advice that we Africans should follow!

My agreement with this family was to take care of two children: Emily, 5, and Bruce, 3. Bruce waited for me at the doorstep with a big smile and welcomed me with a big hug. This gave me a lot of confidence to start my first day of work. Emily was at school and her dad at work. However, Karen, the wife and mother in the family, was available to welcome me, give me a warm hug and offered me something to drink as well.

The God we serve is sovereign: after two years of hardship, without real employment, finally the Lord poured his blessing upon me. My family and I had been in the United States of America since October 2013 and living mainly on our accrued business income and possessions from Belgium and Africa in addition with the support from the work of my elder son Guy-Andre as Translator for companies.

When we arrived the country, efforts were made to secure good secular jobs, but none of the jobs we tried ever led to anything solid. Either we were paid too little or the job was suspended for no reason. Then one day I wondered if God actually wanted me to focus more on the primary motive of our presence in this country; than on ways to earn a living and stop worrying about the next day. It was in this moment of pain that I remembered my testimony!

My Testimony

I remember what God told me the day we suddenly lost our job in Kinshasa, Democratic Republic of Congo. The father of my children, Philippe Pierlot, worked as a teacher at the Gombe Technical School. Of course, as a civil engineer and a professor for the "Belgian Cooperation" he enjoyed a very advantageous financial situation. As for me, I had a business in the ready-to-wear industry and owned a high-end hair salon.

One evening, we learned through the Congolese television news program that the Head of State at the time, President Mobutu Sese Seko, had decreed the immediate departure of any Belgian Aid Worker present on Congolese soil. We were in absolute shock. Without any notice, and without any psychological preparation, our careers had come to an end abruptly. Moreover, we had no idea what we were going to do or become once in Belgium.

This episode was terrifying for everyone. We had to sell our goods (car, furniture, etc.) in a hurry. We had to be strong morally, mentally and above all spiritually to endure what was happening to us and at the same time be able to project ourselves into a Belgian future that seemed so uncertain. A mathematics teacher we knew, unable to bear the thought of losing his job and suddenly leaving the country in which he had lived for so long, even went so far as to commit suicide. What a sad ending.

At that time, I was still in the early stages of my Christian life. So when this sudden disruption occurred, in a flash of the moment, I thought that the world had stopped and that the end was close for me. What was I going to do in Belgium? I didn't even know anyone there. I hated its cold weather, the lack of warmth of its people, and the fact that I had to leave my family to the unknown. Since racism was very real in those days, how was I going to be able to find a job that would suit me and as well stay active professionally? In short, it was a real disaster.

Among the Belgian Aid Workers, the panic was total. Uncertainty, fear and dismay had taken hold of everyone. Even when they already knew that most of them would benefit from the so-called "social reintegration", which is the guarantee by the State of obtaining a job once in Belgium; one thing was sure, however: all would lose the staggering wages they were earning in Africa. Goodbye to servants, lavish lifestyles, restaurants, travels and so on! Once in the Kingdom of Belgium, they would have to tighten their belts and be careful with every penny.

As for me, the tiny, young and with little experience of life African lady, what was I going to become in this country where I thought I had to stay all my life? That was majorly my concern, but God has a plan.

CHAPTER THREE

GOD HAS A PLAN

As I was experiencing a loss of my bearings, I came across a flyer-like "treaty" written by the French pastor, Jean-Louis Jayet in the room of the nanny who was babysitting my children. I was convinced my hands were guided by the Spirit of God to find it. He guides us, He consoles us, enlightens us and places us in paths charted by Him. He speaks to us sometimes in one way, sometimes in another, His ways are not our ways, and His thoughts are not our thoughts, says the word of God in Isaiah 55:9.

I was going to understand many years later that even this hasty and cataclysmic departure-by the fear of the future it caused-was ultimately part of a wonderfully orchestrated plan by God for my life. The treaty included words like:

> *"Why do you worry about the next day?*
> *The next day will worry about itself. Every*
> *day has enough trouble of its own."* (Matthew
> 6:34)

All of sudden I heard an inner voice saying to me, **"Everything you have, everything you possess, your success, did not depend on your abilities, nor the intelligence or assets of the father of your children. But I, God, have done all this for you."**

At that very moment, I was filled with an incredible peace, the fear I had entertained left me completely, and I was convinced that we would be better off in Europe than in Africa.

Regarding this verse, what we must understand and what I have understood and experienced in my Christian walk, is that all we have comes from God. That is why there is no reason for us to look down on people if today our situation seems more enviable or superior than theirs. Instead, we must receive everything with gratitude and thanks-giving. This will bring us closer to God and make us able to share what we have with others if necessary. The Bible says in **Ecclesiastes 11:6:**

> *"Sow your seed in the morning, and*
> *at evening let your hands not be idle,*

for you do not know which will succeed, whether this or that, or whether both will do equally well."

The first two verses of the same chapter say,

"Ship your grain across the sea; after many days you may receive a return.
Invest in seven ventures, yes, in eight; you do not know what disaster may come upon the land."

Give, share, help, support, console, listen... are the many seeds we have sown in our lives and their fruits will benefit our children, grandchildren, great-grandchildren when the time comes. The Bible says,

"Give and it will be given to you."

Believe me when I tell you that this word has been particularly true in my life. I received countless great spiritual, material, moral and emotional blessings in Belgium.

What matters in life is not the place we live in or the people we surround ourselves with, but the *grace* and the *favor* of God. He is the Master of EVERYTHING. He is God, He is the "I am", the one who created all things on this earth, above the earth and below the earth. TRUST in Him and you will be amazed, pleasantly surprised and impressed!

It was in Belgium first, and later in other countries, that I experienced a true social and spiritual elevation. The different countries, cities and islands I had visited have always welcomed me with great consideration, respect and certain expectations. The Lord has covered me with a specific and special grace. People believe in me, or rather in the message of the Gospel that I bring to them. This is the feedback that I have consistently received from many people wherever I have been, and for this I am grateful.

I'm Grateful

At the "Africa, Rise!" conference in Kigali, Rwanda, a Lady Evangelist from Uganda was asked to speak just before I was called up to preach. She turned to me and said, "This lady preaches what she knows, and there is a connection between the Word she teaches and her heart," before adding: "She is true to what she is and to her message."

I realized that people read us and truly understand who we are. The Bible says that the Spirit of the Lord Jesus Christ testifies to us. If you're wrong, know that people see it and know it. Whether you are righteous or unjust, humble or proud, credible or not, honest or lying, corruptible or incorruptible, thief or righteous, good or bad, people watch in silence. However, know that one day your seed will be planted in the ground and you will harvest according to who you are.

Back to My USA Encounter

Let me now go back to the family I used to work for in the United States of America, where God sent me and my children. I want to categorically declare to the glory of God that He has amazed me, and I'm short of words to describe and glorify Him. That position I held and the salary I was given filled my soul with joy, happiness, incredible peace and assurance. Have you ever learned that with our Creator the words "never" and "impossible" are supposed to be banished from your vocabulary?

This is because with Him anything and everything is possible. There are moments, places, circumstances where indeed everything – and I mean absolutely EVERYTHING – suggests that we can't do it, we can't get it back, and we can't fix it. But the Bible says:

- With God everything is possible.
- With Him we will perform exploits

- He who believes in Him will do greater works than Christ Himself
- Greater is He that is in me than he that is in the world
- With God we are more than victorious
- He renews our strength as we walk
- The Lord fights for us, so let's not fear anything
- We are under the shadow of the Almighty
- The Eternal God is our shepherd, we will not lack anything
- He anointed our heads with oil in front of our adversaries, contemplated how our cup is overflowing with blessings and our table is set by the Good Provider with succulent dishes
- Take delight in the Lord and He will fulfill the desires of your heart.

"Anything is possible for the one who believes in this wonderful God and in His son Jesus Christ." (Mark 9:23).

Mark 16:15 *"Then He said to them, 'Go into all the world and preach the Gospel to all creation'."*

Acts 1:8b *"...you will be my witnesses in Jerusalem, and in all Judea and Samaria, and to the ends of the earth."*

I can boldly attest, proclaim and confess to the glory of God that I am among His witnesses. I have seen Him at work in different areas of my life since my conversion in September 1982, when I was just a young student. Jesus Christ is real, and His Word is truth. He truly is the bread of life. Whoever eats it finds true happiness. He is the living water; anyone who drinks it will never be thirsty again. The hunger and thirst for useless, futile, pagan and worldly things are no longer in us and we understand clearly now the words of the Preacher in Ecclesiastes Chapter 1:2 *"Vanity of vanities, all is vanity."*

The race for power and honors loses all meaning. The Bible declares in **2 Corinthians 12:9:** *"...My grace is sufficient for you, for my power is made perfect in weakness. Therefore, I will boast all the more gladly about my weaknesses, so that Christ's power may rest on me..."* In verse **10b:** *"... when I'm weak, then I'm strong..."*

I have recently discovered that certain graces or breakthroughs can only happen to us if we are prepared to receive them. I would also like to say that *what you are* and *what you do* today prepare and shape the way for *what you will be* and *will do* tomorrow. That is why it is imperative that you do everything today as honestly and seriously as possible. If you are on a bad track and you are poorly surrounded, change your environment now, don't wait! Always remember this:

- It is possible to rectify the course of your life
- It is possible to be restored if you have been destroyed or abused.

Wear Fruit, more than just a Label

On my job mentioned earlier, I told my employer that I liked reading and writing and therefore asked them if they would allow me to engage in these two activities during break on my workday. The lady told me that she was absolutely fine with it and that it would push her six year-old daughter Emily to follow my example.

One day, that little girl who was on school vacation, accompanied her maternal grand-mother to a pottery internship. Meanwhile, I agreed with her three year-old brother, Bruce, to teach him a recipe for soup and fresh spinach. At the end of the day, my boss came to sit down with me and we started to talk. We spoke about faith and I asked her if she was born again.

[Editor's Note: What was her answer? Was she born again or did she give her life to Christ in the process?]

Why the question? Simply because I had found that she was behaving like a good Christian, that is, as someone who bears fruits worthy of the Christian walk. She was kind, respectful, humble, polite, generous and grateful for the work I did with her children and her family. She also prayed with her children and helped the poor. If I felt so fulfilled in my workplace, it was largely thanks to the admirable behavior of this couple. Indeed, her husband was the same. I bless them in the name of Jesus. They are the subject of my daily prayers.

Understand that God can raise intercessors on your behalf who beg and cry out to God to open heaven in your favor. They don't know I'm praying for their families. I ask for their business to be fruitful and expand, for the couple to grow in love, harmony, understanding and happiness and that their children grow up with the fear of God.

Sow and Reap your Fruit!

I found great pleasure to come every morning to my workplace, which was already in itself a great blessing because, as we read in **Ecclesiastes 2:24**:

> **"A person can do nothing better than to eat and drink and find satisfaction in their own toil. This too, I see, is from the hand of God..."**

Earning a good salary is great. Enjoying good pay and REJOICING in what you do is priceless. Not to mention, of course, the joy and comfort it brings to your family.

Can I give you another piece of advice? Sow again and again! Don't ever stop! Beyond the strict aspect of money, you can also sow in:

- Peace
- Joy
- Kindness
- Respect
- Loyalty
- Supporting others
- Helping those in need
- Goodness
- Listening
- Honesty
- The truth
- Generosity
- Your given word

Remember that everything we are and do is a seed whether good or bad. At the right time, we'll eat its fruits.

It's almost scary now to publicly give great testimonies in front of Christians because experience has shown us that such testimonies are not always going to please everybody. Instead of rejoicing, some will be so consumed by hatred that they will even be ready to leave the church. This reminds me of an anecdote I fully described in the next chapter.

CHAPTER FOUR

THE SEEDS OF JEALOUSY

In 2006, I purchased a new car, a superb black Mitsubishi truck, a car that had everything for itself, elegance and class. Arriving on Sunday at Grace Upon Grace church, of which I am the founder and sentinel, I said to myself: "If I do not give the testimony, they will not be happy. And if I give the testimony some won't be happy either." It so happened however, that it was not all the members that were negatively affected, of course, it was just a single individual.

To outside onlookers, parking our cars on the street near the church, made some people to believe that we were receiving a big time politician as a guest in our midst. It was unbelievable to them that someone from our own assembly could be able to buy such a car.

After the service, I learned that one of them on getting to know I owned the car looked up on the internet how much the vehicle cost. As a result, she complained to others about why I felt compelled to make such a purchase instead of giving all that money to the poor. Remember Judas' words to Jesus about the woman who poured perfume on his feet in **Mark 14:3-9:**

> *"While he was in Bethany, reclining at the table in the home of Simon the Leper, a woman came with an alabaster jar of very expensive perfume, made of pure nard. She broke the jar and poured the perfume on his head.*
>
> *Some of those present were saying indignantly to one another, 'Why this waste of perfume?*
>
> *It could have been sold for more than a year's wages and the money given to the poor.' And they rebuked her harshly.*
>
> *'Leave her alone,' said Jesus. 'Why are you bothering her? She has done a beautiful thing to me.*
>
> *The poor you will always have with you, and you can help them any time you want. But you will not always have me.*
>
> *She did what she could. She poured perfume on my body beforehand to prepare for my burial.*

> **Truly I tell you, wherever the gospel is preached throughout the world, what she has done will also be told, in memory of her.'"**

I was appalled and scared by what happened because it meant that that person stopped by the car and took the time to write down with great details the specifications of the car in order to refine the research of its price. Her plan was to turn the other members of the church against me, their pastor. It seems like we sometimes have deranged people in our congregations. I'm not afraid to say it. And that's scary. I worked as a pastor in that church without receiving a salary for twenty years. God only knows that I have put all my money into His work. This act had strongly challenged me as to the nature of the people with whom we laugh, we drink, we eat and how insensitive they can be sometimes.

When you behave like that, who are you hurting? Yourself! To investigate the price of my car, surely some form of hatred, jealousy and wickedness was consuming that person mentioned earlier. Do you think that this act prevented me from feeling well and blessed while riding my car? No, quite the contrary. Despite all, I would drive around anyone who needed a ride.

What Do you Have that you haven't Received from God?

Everything we have must be used to the service of others. Our possessions are a blessing not only for ourselves, our family and our friends, but it is for our neighbor also that God visits our storage so that in return we can be a source of blessing for others. Doesn't the Word declare that there is more joy to give than to receive?

Give your time, help others, listen, transport those who cannot move on their own, feed the hungry, clothe those who don't even have anything to wear, financially support those in need. The Word of God declares in **Ecclesiastes 11:1-2, 6**:

> *"Ship your grain across the sea; after many days you may receive a return.*
>
> *Invest in seven ventures, yes, in eight; you do not know what disaster may come upon the land.*
>
> *Sow your seed in the morning, and at evening let your hands not be idle, for you do not know which will succeed, whether this or that, or whether both will do equally well."*

Don't get tired of doing good to others. Give and it will be given to you.

Another advice: don't expect recognition from those you do good to. They may even be the first to criticize you or minimize what you do for them. Consider that it is for God that you do this and that He alone is your reward no matter the situation. At the right time, He will send you "His raven" with the mission of delivering what you need. The raven can be used and sent in different ways by God. I experienced this several years ago in the desert of Air in the Sahara.

CHAPTER FIVE

A WAY IN YOUR DESERT

In 2002-2003, Philippe, the father of my children and I went on holiday to Niger, first to Niamey (capital city of Niger) and then to Agadez (largest city in central Niger). We rented a robust 4 x 4 truck to go on an adventure for a few days in the desert. The idea of living that experience excited me. Of course, I also realized that there might have been people who got lost there or even ended up losing their lives when they couldn't find their way back.

For those of you who don't know, there is no road or path in the desert. Our guide rather followed his own instincts in leading us through the wilderness. And even if there was a path, sandstorms would quickly sweep it away and erase all traces of it.

But back to my testimony. When we reached the middle of the desert, our vehicle broke down, making it impossible for us to go any further. Panic gradually took hold of the entire group. The driver, who was also the guide we had hired in Niamey and the father of my children knew about mechanics.

On that trip, there were four of us: the guide, Philippe, the wife of an ex-student of Philippe-who were our hosts in Niamey-and me.

While the two men were trying to find out the reason for the breakdown and repair the fault, the lady and I went to set up the fire-the "old school" way, given the circumstances-and prepared a baby goat that we had bought earlier in the village. The concern was real because we had no idea how to get out of that situation. Indeed, no one could locate us, cell phones as we know them today did not exist at the time, same for GPS.

Oddly enough, I was perfectly calm, because I was convinced that the Almighty God would send us a crow. So I said to the lady, who happened to be Muslim that Jesus was going to take care of us and send his raven. I was convinced of that. I added that in Elijah's case, the raven sent by God was tasked with bringing him meat. As far as we were concerned, on the other hand, we already had meat; our crow had to be a driver in a vehicle, which would miraculously pass by to rescue us. "God will do it, I'm sure," I told her.

The Crow is on its Way

We continued to prepare the dinner, and I took the opportunity to tell her about the gospel of Christ. I believe I then gave her the testimony of my conversion. Philippe then came to suggest the only realistic solution given the situation we were in. This was that two people would have to walk back to find a village and ask for help, while the other two would stay to keep watch over the rental vehicle.

I refused and categorically rejected that proposal "in the name of Jesus". I found it very risky in every aspect. Indeed, walking under a deadly sun, on roads that do not exist and therefore without any clear direction, while leaving me alone with the guide was an all too dangerous option.

So I said with authority and confidence that I'd die on the spot alongside Philippe rather than endure some horrible death in these hostile sands of the Sahara. I kept on pleading my case insisting that I *knew* and *felt* that a "crow was going to be sent to us by this God I serve."

When one has a real relationship of intimacy with God the Father, God the Son and God the Holy Spirit, it is in the most critical moments, when no rational way out seems possible, that the person involved realizes that he or she no longer reasons according to the prevailing circumstances. An extraordinary peace then floods that heart, for he or she knows that the Creator of the universe is on His way with a solution.

The Bible declares that He is the Master of times and circumstances. There is *nothing* He doesn't know. He has the power to talk to mountains, oceans, wind, sun, moon, stars, forest animals, fish, air, storms and to men and women too. For everything is part of *His* creation of which He is the ultimate Sovereign. Have we not all read this passage in **Jonah 1:17:**

> *"Now the LORD provided a huge fish to swallow Jonah, and Jonah was in the belly of the fish three days and three nights..."*

The same God who brought the fish with the mission of swallowing Jonah is the one who will order that it vomit him after hearing the prayer of the same Jonah. In **Jonah 2:10:**

> *"And the LORD commanded the fish, and it vomited Jonah onto dry land."*

In this case, God gave two commands to the fish: vomit Jonah, and specifying exactly where to spit him out (the land). It is certain that by throwing him into the ocean-given the distress of his heart and the physical fatigue accumulated on his way out of the belly of the fish-Jonas would have surely drowned. But God is omniscient; He knew that the earth was the ideal place for his deliverance. Furthermore, we read in the book of **Jonah 2:1-9:**

> *"From inside the fish Jonah prayed to the LORD his God.*
>
> *He said: 'In my distress I called to the LORD, and he answered me. From deep in the realm of the dead I called for help, and you listened to my cry.*
>
> *You hurled me into the depths, into the very heart of the seas, and the currents swirled about me; all your waves and breakers swept over me.*
>
> *I said, 'I have been banished from your sight; yet I will look again toward your holy temple.'*
>
> *The engulfing waters threatened me, the deep surrounded me; seaweed was wrapped around my head.*
>
> *To the roots of the mountains I sank down; the earth beneath barred me in*

forever. But you, LORD my God, brought my life up from the pit.

When my life was ebbing away, I remembered you, LORD, and my prayer rose to you, to your holy temple.

"Those who cling to worthless idols turn away from God's love for them.

But I, with shouts of grateful praise, will sacrifice to you. What I have vowed I will make good. I will say, 'Salvation comes from the LORD.'"

CHAPTER SIX

CLAIM YOUR DELIVERANCE!

Know that we have a loving, compassionate and merciful God. I urge you to take a few minutes to think about the events and circumstances you have been through, and in which you have felt lost, confused, even hopeless. Start invoking the Eternal God and tell Him that He is the one who can control everything. That He has the answer to your situation. Ask Him for His peace that surpasses all comprehension and He will grant it to you.

Claim the tranquility of your soul and rest will be granted to you by the Master of times and circumstances. The Bible says in **Isaiah 30:15: "This is what the Sovereign LORD, the Holy One of Israel, says: "In repentance and rest is your salvation, in quietness and trust is your strength..."**

Yes, my brother, my sister who read this: you will cry no more! He will grant His grace when you cry! The moment He hears you, He will respond to you as we read in Isaiah 30:19-20:.

> *"People of Zion, who live in Jerusalem, you will weep no more. How gracious he will be when you cry for help! As soon as he hears, he will answer you.*
>
> *Although the Lord gives you the bread of adversity and the water of affliction, your teachers will be hidden no more; with your own eyes you will see them."*

The story of Jonah came to my mind to show you that God is the one who **gives order to all things and to all people to deliver you, to bless you, to save you, to heal you and to free you.**

Let us simply know that He is God. Your case and mine differ from Jonah's, but we have this in common that we all need divine intervention for our freedoms. God will intervene, He has done it in the past, He will do it again. All we have to do is keep hoping in Him, expect from Him and observe His precepts, be and do what He says through His Word.

The Word of God aims to nourish our soul and communicate faith, strength and peace to hang in when things go wrong. Therefore, we will hold on and continue to walk in **His** footsteps. No matter how long the night is, the sun will rise at dawn. Your problems will not last forever, and I command them to leave you now in the name of Jesus! Therefore, endeavor to:

- Have some rest
- Call your joy back where it belongs
- Recover your strength and be dynamic
- Enterprise incessantly
- Let new ideas pop up in your mind for the rebuilding of what has been destroyed
- Bring the laughter back
- Let your face shine
- May those who cause you trouble be confused
- Let the sun shine upon your life. Amen!

Seize your Deliverance

The Bible says in **Isaiah 9:1** *"...there will be no more gloom for those who were in distress..."* Seize your deliverance and breakthrough! Decide to enjoy it now, as you read these lines, **not tomorrow!** On the cross, Jesus Christ accomplished everything. If you are born again, that is, if you accepted Christ in your life, in your heart, as your Savior, Lord and Master, know that you have everything in Him. EVERYTHING!

And I mean every word in that statement. I have experienced each of the things described in these pages. Christ is real and His Word is truth; He is what He says He is and **He accomplishes what He promises.** All we need is to be in harmony with His precepts, place our hope and trust in Him. I have seen Him take *concrete* actions in every aspect of my life. When I met Christ, He spoke to me so clearly that His words have been imprinted in my heart since 1982.

He said:

1. That He loved me-I felt it was a very deep love- and that He would always love me
2. That He was truly resurrected
3. That He was seated at the right of the Father
4. That every time I would go and speak to Him He would hear me and answer me.

The Arrival of Small Clouds

Going back to our episode in the desert. If God had not intervened, we would all have died without a doubt and our bodies would probably have never been found. After all, the Sahara is full of human bones covered by sandstorms, so it's hard to estimate how many tourists have lost their lives there.

Night fell upon us, but my faith level was still at its highest. I was convinced that God would surprise us and send the raven I was talking about earlier, perhaps in the form of a driver in a vehicle that would help us and save us from our distress. After a while, I thought I heard a slight noise coming from far away. I thought in myself, *"Lord, it is like what Elijah said to his servant about the rain that was to fall, and that the latter told him that he would see a small cloud as small as a man's hand. It was enough for a man like Elijah to understand that God heard his prayer and that the rain was on its way."*

When you find yourself in a season of trouble and worry, God will send you, through your prayers, *small clouds* in response to your requests. The sight of these little clouds must be *enough* for you to praise and celebrate your God! The Bible states in **Isaiah 59: 1-2**:

> **"Surely the arm of the Lord is not too short to save, nor his ear too dull to hear. But your iniquities have separated you from your God; your sins have hidden his face from you, so that he will not hear."**

Don't Be a Problem

In that regard, I would like to open a parenthesis. Have you ever realized that the problems faced by Christians are, in most cases, caused by other Christians? Wickedness, jealousy, envy, slander, lies, infidelity, ingratitude, rejection, falsehood, hypocrisy, deceit, cunning, lack of compassion-they're all caused by the same people! And I can continue the list. Let's take a few situations as examples.

If Christians employ you, you'd better pray they'll pay you! Believe it or not, I've seen this too many times. This is dishonest because every worker deserves a salary and if you do not honor your employee, God is watching you and will make you harvest what you've sown.

As Christians, please know that bad things do happen also to good people, so if something bad happens to you, don't expect your brothers and sisters to come and comfort you! On the contrary, you will most likely become the new topic of conversation. Your distress will only get bigger. They would be quite capable of fueling the controversy around your situation to rub it in just a little further.

When the need to discharge the burden of your soul is too great and you go to confide in one of them, be rest assured that your confidant will share it with others, which will cause an even greater sense of betrayal and frustration in you.

Some of you might think I'm exaggerating. I say to you: be honest with yourself, what I am saying is the truth, you have probably experienced it already. Let us repent and Christ will forgive us for our faults and the bad fruits we bear.

My advice is this: **trust in the Lord!** He alone has real compassion, genuine support, true listening, a real solution for you, and the most accurate response to your needs. He's listening to us 24/7 and He wants us well. Give Him the first place in your life and you'll see how things will turn around to your advantage.

Make Him your priority and you will testify on how He treats you as His priority in every aspect of your existence. These two ingredients that I give you are two great secrets for a fulfilled and successful life-a true life of happiness. If you want to know more about this happiness, I invite you to read my next book, *"Rebuild On The Ruins, It's Possible"* which will deal exclusively with this subject.

CHAPTER SEVEN

THE RAVEN HAS COME

On that night of 2002 in the middle of the Sahara in that Desert of Air, we were about to sleep under the stars. Everyone had set up their tent. After supper around the fire, we made sure to put out the blaze so that the flames, driven by the very powerful night winds of the desert, did not burn our small plastic tents.

Suddenly, we saw a 4 x 4 vehicle heading in our direction. The driver stopped some 200 feet away from us. I immediately understood that God alone could have sent him to us. After disembarking his tourists, the driver came to start a discussion with us and asked us what was going on. We explained our situation, and he said, **"At one point, when I was driving, I felt I had to drive here."**

I can't remember exactly my answer to that statement, but knowing myself, I probably said something like, "I prayed that God should send us someone, and He did."

I just wanted to testify to the greatness of my God. They were all Muslims and it was an opportunity to evangelize and proclaim that Christ is listening to us, that He miraculously intervenes in our lives! Amen!

Take every opportunity to testify about Him. Paul said that we should testify and evangelize whether in good or bad circumstances. It is our lifestyle that prevents us from sharing our faith in Jesus. There is a disconnect between our supposed faith and what we really are and do. Our behavior speaks for itself; it attests to whom we really belong to: Christ or the world. You may choose to be hot or cold but remember that God will vomit the lukewarm.

The Bible tells us in **Revelation 2** about the letter written to the Church of Ephesus, in verses **2 to 5:**

> *"I know your deeds, your hard work and your perseverance. I know that you cannot tolerate wicked people, that you have tested those who claim to be apostles but are not and have found them false.*
>
> *You have persevered and have endured hardships for my name, and have not grown weary.*
>
> *Yet I hold this against you: You have forsaken the love you had at first.*

> *Consider how far you have fallen!*
> *Repent and do the things you did at first.*
> *If you do not repent, I will come to you and*
> *remove your lamp-stand from its place."*

Let the Holy Spirit Do His Job

Everything I write comes to me by prophetic inspiration. The reason for it is that every sentence of this book is personally addressed to you the reader. Take the time to reflect, and ask the Holy Ghost to enlighten you for your deliverance, in the name of Jesus. Read every biblical passage presented, meditate on them, study them, and the Spirit will open your eyes and intelligence to grasp its depth for your life and your Christian walk.

The Holy Ghost is not a fiction, He is real. He communicates wisdom, intelligence and know-ledge to us. He opens our eyes so that we may see and understand the mysteries hidden to the wise men of this world. Let Him remind you of the prophecies spoken unto your life for which you have not grasped the depth yet. Remember how you felt on the day of your conversion to Christ and return through faith to the path of the promises you made to your Lord and Savior. May the Spirit give you the strength to stand up and move forward!

I recall my encounter with the Muslim woman, as we were preparing a fire in the sand on that special night, the way the people of the desert normally do. That night, I said to God in the depths of my soul: "In this situation, may Your will be done." I had gone on this journey with a heart filled with excitement and enthusiasm for several reasons:

1. I wanted to understand some spiritual realities found in the Bible about wells in the desert
2. Jesus Himself was led into the desert after his baptism
3. I wanted to understand what the oasis represented.

There were also other "earthly" motivations such as seeing camel caravans carrying goods, meeting the "blue men" (the Tuareg people) and seeing them at work, or learning more about the ways of life in the desert.

Your Will, not Mine

God knew how much I wanted to live all these experiences and go through with this journey. Despite this, I told Him in that prayer that His will should prevail. If He decided to end everything right there, I would accept it, even if I personally wanted to continue. Nothing happens to us by accident. The Lord is Master of our lives, He leads us *the way* He wants, *where* He wants, *with whom* and *when* He wants!

Are you currently in serious trouble? Know that He does not ignore it! This situation has been going on for some time now? He knows it! Are you weeping over your fate? He hears you, He sees you! **Romans 8: 28-29** says:

> *"And we know that in all things God works for the good of those who love him, who have been called according to his purpose.*
>
> *For those God foreknew he also predestined to be conformed to the image of his Son, that he might be the firstborn among many brothers and sisters."*

Our attitude in times of distress is of great importance in the eyes of God. Remember Job and all the misfortunes that have struck him. If he was able to get double of what he owned before his trials, it is obvious that it was his attitude that made the difference.

On a Divine Commando Mission to the Muslims.

The next day after we were rescued in the desert, the driver took us to a nearby village. Of course, he took advantage of our misfortune to charge us a staggering "rescue fee". We had not much choice, this is the world we live in; one takes advantage of the poor when they can't defend themselves.

Arriving in the village, I understood that our breakdown was in fact God's plan **for a specific mission among its Muslim inhabitants.** In the evening, I asked to be taken to visit a group of young boys I had met during the day. I set an appointment for them around 7:00 p.m. Night was falling and we were all gathered in a hut. I began to tell them about Jesus Christ, the Savior, the one who heals, blesses, delivers, brings happiness, opens intelligence and gives meaning to our lives.

I was testifying enthusiastically over and over again. The idea that those young Muslims could convert gave me zeal and courage. I could feel my faith grow. The boys were all the time with me. They eventually accepted and confessed Jesus as their Lord and Savior. We were all so happy and we enjoyed every single minute we spent together.

They taught us how to cook bread on the sand, and asked me different questions. We all also went together to Mr. Soule's garden where we had fun. I saw the seed in them and I am sure that the Holy Spirit watered them. Thank you Jesus.

CHAPTER EIGHT

WORSHIP IN MISFORTUNE

My soul is overwhelmed by a well-being that is difficult to describe with words. I wake up in the morning with happiness in my heart, I spend my days remembering the blessings and the goodness of God, and I lie down in the night with songs of praise and joy. I don't have the words to express my gratitude to *my* God. My love for the Holy Ghost is tenfold because I realize that everything is the work of His hands, everything is the result of His intervention. There is a song that says:

I miss the words
To praise You, to worship You
Oh, Jesus!

Another inspired song says this:

Hail Jesus! You're my King!
Your life frees me to sing

I will praise You all of my days
You're perfect in all Your ways
Glory, glory to the Lamb
Glory, glory to Jesus

I suddenly feel praise and worship overwhelm my soul. New songs rise in my heart in gratitude to the One who is *my* God. My mind takes me several years back, during my trip to Rwanda. Following a misfortune that had struck my family, I found myself completely disoriented and in a state of extreme pain. Despite the pain, which seemed incurable at the time, I was invited to teach in Pastor Josephine's "*Victory Church*" in Kanombe, a neighborhood in the capital of Rwanda. Every night for a week I preached to support and contribute to this beautiful work started by Pastor Josephine.

But in the very same period of my life, I found myself at the bottom of the valley of the shadow of death, in a state of panic and depression such that there was no hope or solution for me to see on the horizon. I had been having great difficulty expressing my feelings since the beginning of May 2015. I even came to beg the Holy Ghost to give me words and expressions to say the growing gratitude that sprang and flooded my heart when I thought of Him.

This gratitude, of course, came from the great surprise gift that Heavenly Father gave me with my work. In November 2012, God spoke to me several times **that He would make a way "in my desert"** (Isaiah 43). I did not understand the reason for this revelation, since at that time I was experiencing happiness at every level-family, finances, ministry, projects, etc.

The Valley of Tears

However, a few months after this message, I truly began a journey through the desert that lasted about three years. Like Nehemiah I continued to primarily take care of everything related to the Kingdom of God with one hand, and wiped away my tears with the little strength left in me with the other hand.

As far as I can remember, I had never cried so much in my life. Moreover, praying on my knees had become so frequent and long that I realized one day that they were badly damaged. My panic was such that it was now visible on my face. When I looked in the mirror, I felt like I was looking at someone else. I begged God to give me back my true face, to become, by His power, "me again". I do not wish this for anybody, not even my worst enemies. Unhappiness kills you slowly, it eats you away, it disfigures and makes you ugly.

I prayed with faith and authority for the relief of my face from death. And it is with joy that I can tell you today that God has answered me. Not only did He restore the natural state of my face, but He made it brighter than before. I saw myself rejuvenated and I even regained the dynamism of yester years. Courage and audacity are my allies in battle again!

Indeed, on top of the deterioration of my face, I had lost 95% of my hair, just like people with cancer do. I begged God, the One who says in His Word that He knows the number of our hair on our head. Again, He restored me and my dignity.

How can we not praise Him, worship Him, serve Him and be a witness to the world for Him? He's amazing. My love belongs to Him, my adoration belongs to Him, and my happiness is perfected in Him.

CHAPTER NINE

BARY'S MINISTRIES CHURCH BABY STEPS IN THE UNITED STATES OF AMERICA (USA)

When I arrived at my workplace early July 2015, the atmosphere really improved compared to the previous days. And there was a good reason for it.

Three days earlier, we officially properly conducted our first service at *Bary's Ministries Church* in the United States, in accordance with the mandate God gave us three years before. At last, the purpose for our departure from Europe was fulfilled. And just like that I led our first worship service on July 5, 2015 at 1:30 p.m. in the city of Euless, Texas.

We bless God for the success of the opening; the Lord was truly present in the praise and worship, as well as in the preaching. I want to bless all those who supported us and helped to make the program a success. I bless my eldest son, Guy-André, who continues to support and give 100% to the work and ministry that God has entrusted to me since 1993. He started at the age of thirteen on the drums, and has since then done the ministry silently and discretely. Our presence in the USA is largely due to Him and His role in all administrative procedures.

I am proud of my second son, Roland Pierlot who also started helping us in Belgium at age thirteen serving in the Sunday School for kids, and playing keyboard. When he moved back to Belgium, he provided us a very good and invaluable support for the church and our family. He is calm and strong as he does important things for us in silence and with enviable discretion.

The Devil is a Liar

At the same time, the past two weeks had been terrible at work and I was under constant attacks. The devil is a liar, I know it, and the Bible also reminds us of that. Indeed, seeing that I was experiencing success after success, victory after victory, testimony after testimony, and that all my being was overflowing with happiness and joy, there was no way the devil could sit back and watch.

When the place of worship was granted to us, I started to have all kinds of night visions in which I was attacked in different ways. Our enemy has already failed two thousand years ago, but he is been relentless. When one of his plans fails, he comes back with another one. But our faith and perseverance defeat him and we are more than victorious by the name of Jesus!

And so that morning the atmosphere at work was very good. Good mood, jokes, mutual trust back in track, laughter, complicity. Yet we came a long way with my employer. There is a time to cry, but there is also a time to rejoice. Just pay attention to how you behave in your testing season.

Hope after the Storm

When a favorable season arrives in your life, learn to savor every moment of grace and favor bestowed upon you by the Eternal God. Testify, rejoice, laugh, dance, praise and sing, for the Eternal God has remembered you. He is faithful and He never forgets his own! He allows us to go through trials in order to train and carve us out to get the shape He wants us to reach so that we can grow spiritually. **John 15:1-5**

> *"I am the true vine, and my Father is the gardener.*

He cuts off every branch in me that bears no fruit, while every branch that does bear fruit he prunes so that it will be even more fruitful.

You are already clean because of the word I have spoken to you.

Remain in me, as I also remain in you. No branch can bear fruit by itself; it must remain in the vine. Neither can you bear fruit unless you remain in me.

"I am the vine; you are the branches. If you remain in me and I in you, you will bear much fruit; apart from me you can do nothing."

How could you fully understand compassion if you did not personally go through severe problems that required the intervention of a Good Samaritan in your life to help you and bandage your wounds? It is only since our arrival in the USA that I have experienced what we commonly call "faith" in its full dimension.

CHAPTER TEN

LIVING AND EXPERIENCING THE WORD OF GOD

Believe me, much of what we read in the Bible can remain in the field of reading and literary analysis. But to move from literature to palpable and concrete reality, to something we can see, touch and feel then we have to go through a series of life experiences that fall within the field of trial and testing. Sometimes you have to go through fire to know how much it burns and how badly it can hurt.

Fortunately, however, the Lord tells us in his Word in Isaiah 43:2 that even if we went through the fire, the flames would not consume us. In other words, the trials will not overcome us **because the Lord crosses them with us.** Let us place our trust in Him and continue to hope for His deliverance and His divine intervention. That's why we shouldn't complain. As the song says:

Fear not, The Lord is for you

No, don't be afraid, He's taking care of you.

The Lord will fight for you,

Yes, he'll fight for you.

Amen!

The same Word of God also declares that,

"They will wage war on you, but they will not defeat you."

During that period, I lived spiritual battles that materialized in the physical world, in a very concrete way in my everyday life, and at my workplace in particular.

But it did not frighten me at all, for He who is in me is stronger than he who is in the world fighting me. Obviously, the church we opened disturbed the invisible and nefarious world. How so?

- Indeed, my salary allowed us to think and set up ambitious new projects here in the United States.
- Because the establishment of *Bary's Ministries Church* was a divine mission and mandate for which we had left everything in Europe and took all sorts of risks just for the work of God, it was

obvious that a great spiritual work awaited us. The devil could only be intimidated and annoyed.

- Through my job, I witnessed a special kind of elevation on a moral, psychological, spiritual and material level. Not to mention the many connections I could get through my employer.

For example, they directed me to a car dealership whose owner happened to be a good friend of theirs. And through them, I became the owner of a superb Toyota Avalon, which is a luxury car, at a very competitive price. At the risk of appearing superficial, I felt a great satisfaction at its acquisition. Every time I saw or got in the car, a voice would say to me, "This is the elevation of God!"

Rejoice in the Lord! He's the one who spices up and seasons your life! This testimony about my car is intended to glorify God. Because everything we have comes from Him, even when your finances allow you to obtain everything you need.

As children of God, **we will not be weeping and lamenting forever.** On the contrary, the joy, peace, security and hope belong to us! If we cry through trials, it is so that we may be trained to experience the Father's intervention for us. What-ever the waters you go through, if you cross with Christ, **you will arrive safely.**

The Mystery of God's Love

In mid-July 2015, during my morning prayer, I had a revelation. I was in my bathroom and I realized how extraordinary God is. The Apostle Paul said,

> *"**Who will separate us from Christ's love? Will it be tribulation, or anguish, or persecution, or hunger, or nudity, or peril, or sword?***
>
> *But in all these things we are more than victorious by the one who loved us.*
>
> *For I have the assurance that neither death nor life, nor angels nor dominations, nor present things nor things to come, nor powers, nor height, nor depth, nor any other creature can separate us from the love of God manifested in Jesus Christ our Lord.* "* (Romans 8:35, 37-39)

Also I, Jacqueline Baributsa, His servant, declare:

"NOTHING WILL DETACH OR SEPARATE ME FROM JESUS!" And no matter what I go through, I will testify at all time and in every place to God's FAITHFULNESS to his children and servants.

CHAPTER ELEVEN

BARY'S MINISTRIES CHURCH: WHERE IT ALL BEGAN

On a Sunday of June 2015, I had a meeting with the committee of the *United Memorial Christian Church* who had opened their doors for us to have a worship place in Euless. They wanted to hear from me about *Bary's Ministries,* my calling and mission to the United States. I felt a little discouraged because of how slow their final decision process to give me the green light for the start of *Bary's Ministries Church* was going.

However, I was excited to start the following Sunday. But the idea of having to wait over a month for another council meeting and its unanimous vote in favor of us using their building discouraged me somewhat. I came out of this meeting where some twenty-five people were sitting watching me like one who comes out of an oral exam in college. *Keep quiet and see how the Holy Ghost will act on your behalf.*

As I came through the main hall, Pastor Mary Lou Dillon led me to the committee. I was impressed and intimidated. After a brief introduction, she invited me to take a seat. I could now start talking. So I got up but was neither sure where to start nor what they wanted to hear to be honest:

The committee: *You seem to operate like the Apostle Paul, going from country to country for the ministry.*

Me: *Yes, for we operate in an apostolic call that differs from the missionary call* (in fact, the missionary is sent by the congregation while the apostle is sent by God).

The Committee: *Why did you choose Texas and Euless as the place to build your church?*

Me: *My intimate relationship with God always drives me to obey what He tells me. He said that He was sending us to Dallas/Fort Worth.*

When the interview process concluded, the only thing I could testify of was that as soon as I got up, I felt an **inner authority,** calmness and a gentleness surrounding me. I spoke with self-control and confidence and I knew the Holy Ghost was visiting some of the members of the committee.

God is faithful, and He had made a way. I blessed Him because of how comfortable I was while talking to them. Almost all of them felt like hugging me when we ended the meeting.

After my presentation, the pastor suggested that I would be asked a few questions to better understand my calling and my mission. They had to make their decision to welcome us with as much information as possible at their disposal. The rest now is history.

CHAPTER TWELVE

SOMETHING NEW IN THE AIR

By mid-December 2015, I resolved to fast for a week. Of course, every single special fasting and prayer program I start is always inspired by the Holy Ghost. During this period of fasting, I received several visions. The purpose and reason of these spiritual appointments was simply to "worship God", to tell Him all my gratitude for His love and divine intervention in my life, and the ministry He entrusted to me from 1993 to this day. It was also to tell Him how much His greatness amazed me despite the trials of life.

Immediately after that dry fast, a door was opened for me in Atlanta, where I stayed for almost a month. By the way, that trip was the first after I moved here to Dallas, Texas, from Belgium where I had spent more than half of my life. It was therefore the first door of blessings after the fast.

In Atlanta, I served in two assemblies and was connected to other churches based in Washington DC, New York, Seattle and Houston. My mind attested in me that my apostolic call to America was just starting, and this coming to Georgia was only the premise.

In January 2016, I continued or at least took another time of fasting that I would cut off in the evening allowing myself to eat and drink. I was locked up in prayer for several days and it truly benefited me inwardly. It's a very good spiritual exercise and you always come out of it with countless blessings.

During my time in Atlanta, the Lord also opened my mind to finally make me admit that my eldest son Guy-André was not a mere helper in my ministry and church but an "equal partner" in everything I did for the kingdom of God.

In addition, the Spirit of God made me understand that he was to be the one in charge of *Bary's Ministries Church* here in the United States. I kept this in my mind thinking that one day I would share this with him. Despite this revelation however, I understood that it was a transitional time of training for him towards his apostolic calling. May the Lord be glorified. The titles God give us for His calling are there to accomplish His mission, to build the body of Christ, not to flatter our ego as we read in **Ephesians 4:11:**

> **"So Christ himself gave the apostles, the prophets, the evangelists, the pastors and teachers, to equip his people for works of service, so that the body of Christ may be built up..."**

The Lord gave His servants as gifts to the Church and clothed them with spiritual abilities for a special service. That is why we should not brag about our gifts because they're all at the service of His Church.

A month later, we were back in Dallas. Many servants of God began to prophesy to my son that he was indeed the pastor of *Bary's Ministries Church.* As for me, they said that the Lord would give me further details about His next way to use me in my calling in His Kingdom.

This was only a confirmation of what I had already felt since that December fast. But to tell you the truth, I never wanted my children to become pastors. I told myself that they could do ministry as part of God's work, but being a pastor was not my choice for them.

You might object that it is truly baffling that someone who has been doing the ministry for twenty-six years and traveled the world for the gospel makes that kind of statement. But it is precisely because I see and live through things from the inside that I know the price to pay when serving as a leader. Jealousy, slander, insults, rejection, successive abandonments, rumors, mockery, gratuitous wickedness are our daily bread. These unjust attacks on us come more often than not from the people with whom we have lived, shared and collaborated in God's work. People who even call themselves our spiritual sons and daughters.

Not to mention that some pastors are to be added to this list of people who fight you. It is obvious that this profession is one of the most ungrateful on earth. Today, many men and women of God experience depression and illnesses one could link to these situations of stress and distress. However, know that *"...there will be no more gloom for those who were in distress.... but in the future He will honor..."* (Isaiah 9:1)

If past times have covered you with shame and scorn, know also that the times to come will cover you with glory! Amen! Woe to you if by your wickedness you have been the cause for the suffering of a man or a woman of God. Be careful because the Bible says in **Hebrews 13:17**

> *"Have confidence in your leaders and submit to their authority, because they keep watch over you as those who must give an account. Do this so that their*

work will be a joy, not a burden, for that would be of no benefit to you."

Coming back to the calling of my children, I have come to the conclusion that they belong to God and that we, as parents, are only stewards who must manage them well because we will be accountable to the Lord for them.

Moreover, every parent should pray and wish that only God's perfect will might be done in the lives of their children. God is love and everything that happens to us through Him is a blessing. Even the trials are a great subject of glory when you come out victorious. And your victory will depend on your attitude during the trial and your level of expectation of His divine intervention. Never forget that the Eternal God we serve is FAITHFUL! Amen.

Don't Give Up, Hold On!

Here are some features that define heroes:
- They never give up what they started
- They don't give up even in difficult times
- They don't pay too much attention to those who urge them to give up
- They do not consider the elements that go against their goals

- When they lack strength, they encourage and strengthen themselves and pursue their goals
- They work methodically to achieve their objectives
- They think relentlessly about their goals
- They research and educate themselves to maximize success
- They surround themselves with people who believe in them
- They surround themselves with positive people and therefore remove or distance themselves from pessimistic and negative people
- They partner with courageous and ambitious people
- Their work perfectly serves their objectives
- They speak, walk, live, think, dress and even eat in relation to their aspirations
- Nothing stops them
- They don't see obstacles the same way ordinary people do
- Each obstacle is an opportunity to help them do better and move forward faster
- They have faith in what they aspire to
- They convince themselves that they will be successful
- They can foresee the victory after the fight

I could go on and on with this list. Bottom line is that heroes do not give up and they stand firm regardless of the circumstances, the seasons or the oppositions.

Yes with God we will accomplish more exploits. Through Him, we have the capacity to do so, for He is our source of inspiration, strength, audacity and courage. And He's the one who inspires us in the areas we are called to do those exploits in. There is no doubt that we are called to impact the society we live in and leave a mark for future generations.

There is no arrogance in this statement. On the contrary, it is a completely normal, even banal thing to say. What good would it be to leave this earth without having accomplished something profoundly significant? With Christ in us, anything is possible.

When I talk about doing exploits and impacting society, it is not to get some vain personal glory. Rather, it is to bring about a change, a transformation in the lives of the people around us, whether kin or strangers. How?

- Through our preaching
- Through our work ethic
- Through the writings, books and articles we write and publish
- Through the good life principles we implement
- Through our personal success
- Through our education and career

- Through our discoveries
- Through our talents

All these of course with the sole purpose of glorifying the name of the Lord and in return desiring to be a blessing and an example for our society, our church and our family.

CHAPTER THIRTEEN

WHEN YOUR TIME COMES

In March 2016, my sister Dona from Canada, with great sadness, announced the brutal death of the entire Lapierre family. Mr. Lapierre previously worked for the Canadian government and had a career as a journalist. Apparently he had just lost his father and was on his way to his funeral. He wanted to be by his mother's side to support her in this terrible ordeal.

The family had booked a flight to get to their mother's house as soon as possible. He was travelling with his wife, his two brothers and his sister when the plane crashed. A real tragedy. This man seemed to possess an extraordinary charisma and had impacted the lives of all the people he met. Canada was mourning. His political opponents paid tribute to him, Christians and citizens of other faiths mourned him. They all agreed that this was a huge loss for the country.

He was considered a hero who had left a visible mark in the lives of Canadians and immigrants living in Canada. I hope with all my heart that they belonged to Jesus. Death strikes unexpectedly, which is why we must all, without exception, prepare ourselves to appear clean before the Lord.

What will people say about you when you die? I am not talking about the hypocritical and formal false speeches spoken at the morgue or during the religious service before inhumation. Do you notice that at departing the world of the living, everyone curiously agrees to praise the deceased ones, even when they were the worst individuals who ever walked the earth?

Although it is a universal phenomenon, I have observed it particularly among fellow Africans. Is it hypocrisy or just the fear of the dead? I personally believe that it is better to stay quiet rather than make up qualities they never possessed. Even in times of mourning, let us stay authentic, even if the deceased belonged to our own family.

Never Give Up Because the Best is Yet to Come

Before you do anything, especially if it's important, you have to think carefully and evaluate the cost of any initiative in terms of time, energy, money, etc.

This is why when it comes to business investment; it is required to present a detailed project along with a proper business plan.

So before even starting the implementation of any given project, the preliminaries can already be tedious, even expensive, because everything has to be thought through by experts that will charge you a fee for their service. All these could be done without any guarantee that the project will be accepted by the bank or by any other institution competent to receive and approve it.

But with God, things often happen in a completely different way. Sometimes He inspires us to complete a task and requires a swift execution that does not necessarily follow a logical pattern of action. A personal experience comes to mind.

I have already told you about our painful experience of leaving Congo (formerly Zaire) in 1989, but my desire is to return to Kinshasa for an evangelical mission one day.

Since I was leaving the country for good, I decided to travel to Goma, eastern Congo, to say goodbye to my parents. Only God knew after how many years I was going to be able to see them again. On the day of my return to Kinshasa, at the airport all the passengers had already finished boarding and the plane was in its lane ready to take-off.

Despite my delay, the already closed doors and the engines running at full throttle, an inner voice told me that I had to take this flight no matter what. But how? The voice did not communicate it to me.

God's Inspiration makes us Look Crazy!

The people around me were trying to reason with me and made me understand that I was losing my mind. I did not pay attention to them. In my mind, I could visualize myself on that plane. I told the people who had dropped me at the airport that they could go home with my luggage and that my purse would be more than enough for this travel.

Suddenly I saw employees who were working on the tarmac coming to me. They asked to escort me to the plane because the pilot had ordered the doors of the plane to be opened in order to get me in. I kissed my parents goodbye, took my purse and followed them.

But these employees told me to give them my luggage so they could load it with the rest, because only they were authorized to do so. I think I told them I didn't need to take my luggage because none of them had been checked in. But they insisted that the pilot had specifically given the order to open the baggage hold to put my suitcases in. Is such a thing possible? Yes, it is possible! God is above all, even above the very strict laws governing an airport. I was escorted, I went on the plane, went to my seat next to a white man who looked in absolute shock!

Obey, Even When you Don't Understand

The flight attendants did not understand what was going on. For in the history of aviation, this was certainly unseen or unheard of. But God makes exceptions to the rule with us and for us. I couldn't believe it myself. Thank you, Lord!

Throughout the flight, I was so grateful I couldn't stop crying. I was so amazed that my obedience to this inner voice had turned into an incredibly improbable but beneficial reality to me. Very often when God visits us through His blessings, it is hard to believe what's going on, and we ask ourselves, "How is this even possible?"

Let us learn to listen to what the Holy Ghost tells us, it will allow us to access the inaccessible and train our spiritual ear. I could convince myself that I had missed my flight and that it was better to go home and book another flight for Kinshasa with the travel agency. But that inner voice was so strong and so real that I had to get on *that* plane and not another one. **Never give up,**

and if you have this strong conviction in yourself, don't stop on the way!

If I had acted logically according to the situation, I would never have had the great and beautiful experience of seeing the hand of God moving in that pilot's heart, forcing him to take me on board, even on the tarmac. I later found out that the people of Goma were talking about me saying, "How does this woman deserve such a thing to happen? Her God is great."

Hebrews 11:1 says, "_Now faith is confidence in what we hope for and assurance about what we do not see._"

In **Isaiah 30:21**, the Bible declares,

"_Whether you turn to the right or to the left, your ears will hear a voice behind you, saying, 'This is the way; walk in it.'_"

In verse **18,** it is said,

"_Yet the LORD longs to be gracious to you; therefore he will rise up to show you compassion. For the LORD is a God of justice. Blessed are all who wait for him!_"

Here's what I feel inspired to tell you prophetically. Are you unhappy, discouraged or totally down, and nothing seems to cheer you up? Stand up and speak aloud to your circumstance, to your problem. Tell them:

- The Eternal God will rescue me. He is God, He is good, and He is righteous. He has kept me and supported me until today and he will do it again!
- So "problem/situation" I declare to you now, pack up your stuff and get out of my heart, my house and my family, in the name of Jesus!

Open the door and tell them to get out and never come back. Close the door. Then start praying (in tongues if you can) and receive His peace, in the name of Jesus.

In **Isaiah 30:15** we read that:

> **"In repentance and rest is your salvation, in quietness and trust is your strength, but you would have none of it"** and in **verse 19:**
> **"you will weep no more. How gracious he will be when you cry for help! As soon as he hears, he will answer you."**

May the Lord bless you, your testimony is on the way, already praise the Eternal God for what He's about to do.

A Single Act of Obedience Can Lead to Years of Happiness

Finally, I started my journey from Kisangani, Upper-Zaire and present-day Congo, where I had a layover of a few hours, before continuing to my final destination Kinshasa.

I got home in the evening. Because we were aware we would be leaving the country soon we saw it fit to move to my older sister Domina Baributsa Musoni in the Green City while we waited for our imminent and final departure.

After greeting the whole family and experiencing the joy of my two young sons (one and a half and a three year old), I was told that a man had been there waiting for several hours already. He wanted to buy and take over my business. He was sitting on the porch alone; the others were inside the house.

I suddenly understood why this inner voice had been so insistent that I would not miss this flight. I went to greet him and introduced myself as the owner of the coveted business. It was a high-end, fully equipped hair salon. Let me tell you that I have always favored quality things. Whatever we do, I think it's always good to have quality result or outcome. And I always do the same in the ministry.

He explained how he wanted to buy the business and pay in foreign currency-Belgian francs as far I was concerned-which was obviously music to my ears. I don't remember what state of mind I was in, but knowing myself, I most likely was praying in my heart to get a satisfactory deal.

As the journey to Belgium was approaching, I didn't have the luxury to think about another potential buyer. The one I had on hand was "my manna". But to my surprise, he suddenly replied that he did not want to discuss this matter with a woman and demanded a man to make the deal with. Who would have imagined that as the 21st century was knocking at the door one could still come across this kind of backward mentality? The worst part is that even in the ministry, many pastors also behave the same way. In John 4:4, didn't Jesus Christ Himself have a respectful conversation with the Samaritan woman? And from this dialogue did he not teach us what the Father asked of true worshippers?

In verse 23-24 of the same chapter it reads,

"Yet a time is coming and has now come when the true worshipers will worship the Father in the Spirit and in truth, for they are the kind of worshipers the Father seeks.

God is spirit, and his worshipers must worship in the Spirit and in truth."

I finally was able to convince him that if he was really interested buying the business, the only person in a position to sell it to him was the sole owner of that business, and that's me. Glory to God he had a rethink about it and we finalized the deal. My satisfaction was great especially as the country was going through a very serious financial crisis. How could I not praise my God, He who showed me once again that no one could predict His next move. He does what He likes, He uses whomever He wants and at the time that He seems fit. Hallelujah!

I am convinced that the Holy Ghost had forced this man to stay on that porch so he could wait for me. Why do I say that? For the Lord wanted to bless His daughter and make me live an extraordinary experience that I would never forget. I would later on use it to bear witness to His greatness and power and declare that He is a God above all natural law!

Therefore, I urge you to be obedient. But to achieve this, one must also have a sensitive ear to the voice of the Holy Ghost. And to get to that level, you have to cultivate your relationship with God. How?

- By consistent prayer
- Through the reading of the Bible
- Through regular meditation
- By a consistent study of the Bible
- Through frequent fasting
- By your personal retirement times

Believe me, having an intimate relationship with the Heavenly Father, with Jesus and with the Holy Ghost is such a precious and wonderful thing. It is real, tangible and simply beautiful. When you reach this level of understanding and experience, your life takes a whole new turn. You touch the true meaning of a fulfilled and satisfying life enriched with joy, peace, serenity, security and freedom.

Once we have come to this true and intimate relationship with God-the Father, Son and Holy Spirit-different graces and favors are bestowed upon us. The paths of life seem to be wide open for us and we walk with confidence and flexibility. If some use elbows and low blows to get to the top, you on the other hand

will be assigned an escort that will drive you more slowly perhaps, but surely.

I'm not saying you'll be exempt from hardship, life's problems or all kinds of hassle; on the contrary, you may even experience more tribulations than others. But in this process, you will have one hand that will wipe away your tears and another that you will lift to worship and praise your God. For you will be confident that He will get you out of your distress eventually and that a great testimony will come out from your liberation.

The Word of God declares that unhappiness often reaches the righteous but **that God always delivers him!** And I know what I'm talking about. The ministry has taken me on an emotional rollercoaster trust me. However, if someone is the artisan of your misfortune, I advise you not to return evil to them. For God says,

> *"**Revenge is mine and retribution is mine.**"* (Romans 12:19)

The Bible also states in **Galatians 6:7**

> *"**Do not be deceived: God cannot be mocked. A man reaps what he sows.**"*

Don't try to justify yourself because Christ is the one who justifies us. Similarly, don't speak badly to those who provoke you, insult you, criticize you, and make up fake stories to harm you and mistreat you but *keep quiet.*

> **"The LORD will fight for you; you need only to be still."** (Exodus 14:4)

> **Isaiah 30:15b** *"In repentance and rest is your salvation, in quietness and trust is your strength, but you would have none of it."*

In reality, you have something they don't have. They envy you. That's why they get so agitated when you pass by. But don't stop at their frenzy and follow the path to your destiny. In **Psalm 23:5-6**, King David writes,

> **"You prepare a table before me in the presence of my enemies.**
> **You anoint my head with oil; my cup overflows. Surely your goodness and love will follow me all the days of my life, and I will dwell in the house of the LORD forever."**

Who Can Resist Him?

This buyer ended up changing his macho mentality and bought my business. This event may have happened a long time ago in distant lands, I still benefit from this act of obedience until today. That is why I told you earlier that a simple act of obedience, even of a second, can follow you for the rest of your life and open many doors and lasting graces. It can even follow the generations that will come after you.

The older one of my two children was only three and a half years old at that time, but today both of them are in their thirties and are enjoying the fruits of their mother's obedience to God's voice. I bless God that I knew Him in my youth, I bless Him for making me love Christ madly, and for having given the grace of loving everything that concerns His kingdom. I give Him thanks for He has called me to His service, for He has given me the grace to pray easily for hours, to fast with ease and consistently for years. I exalt Him because I've communicated His love, greatness and mercy with so much freedom. I bless Him for my thirst and hunger for Him; I bless Him for all His interventions in my life, for all His companionship in difficult times. But I also bless God for all the trials I encountered because they have made me a sister, a servant, a woman, a mother with a testimony for the glory of the Almighty. May all that is in me, and all that is mine, bless His holy name! Amen.

I bless my sister Dona Baributsa Ntihi who was the one who mentioned to her friend Adeline that I was selling my business, who in turn mentioned it to the client who eventually bought my business. That was the only marketing done by word of mouth. For this reason, I also express my thanks to Adeline who directed the client to me. Again I say a big "Thank You" to these two servants of God.

CHAPTER FOURTEEN

GOOD STEWARDSHIP

The Bible says, *"What have you that you haven't received?"* (1 Cor. 4:7).

It is important to realize that everything we own comes from God: family, health, work, finances, ministry, knowledge, strength, salvation. God sows in our lives and at some point He will want to harvest. And he expects the crop to be of good quality, of *excellent* quality. May the Eternal God help us through His Spirit to understand this.

We are all debtors to God's, who in His own time will make us accountable for everything He has invested in us. Sooner or later, He will come to us and say, *"What have you done with what I invested in you?"* You remember the parable of the talents in **Matthew 25: 14-19 (KJV)?**

"For the kingdom of heaven is as a man travelling into a far country, who called his own servants, and delivered unto them his goods.

And unto one he gave five talents, to another two, and to another one; to every man according to his several ability; and straightway took his journey.

Then he that had received the five talents went and traded with the same, and made them other five talents.

And likewise he that had received two, he also gained other two.

But he that had received one went and digged in the earth, and hid his lord's money.

After a long time the lord of those servants cometh, and reckoneth with them."

In verse 27, He continues,

"...Thou oughtest therefore to have put my money to the exchangers, and then at my coming I should have received mine own with usury." (KJV)

*"Well then, you should have put my money on deposit with the bankers, so that when I returned I would have received it back with **interest**." (NIV)*

If you read the rest on your own from verse 20 to 30 you'll see how the other two servants who made their talents grow have each earned a double portion of what they were given originally.

Good management of assets is not mere administrative knowledge or accounting skills. It is a state of mind, a mindset, a general principle, a way of functioning. Let us therefore not neglect what we have in hand and unnecessarily waste it.

Don't Worry About Anything

When I left for Europe permanently, I didn't see how I could ever be successful in that new environment. How a tiny lady with young children like me could possibly make it on that allegedly racist continent, in that cold and rainy country, without any family, without friends, without any hobby, without any church? How could she make it in this new world? I was completely over-whelmed. But God is faithful.

Before I left Africa, He had made me to understand by revelation that He was the author of my every success in life, and that it had nothing to do with my business skills. It was also from this experience that He made me realize the full dimension of the passage in **Matthew 6:34:**

> *"Therefore do not worry about tomorrow, for tomorrow will worry about itself. Each day has enough trouble of its own."*

The Greek word translated as "punishment" implies grief, adversity, misfortune or calamity. As soon as I received this revelation, I got completely free, and the fear of the great departure and uncertain tomorrows left me instantly. The One who had given me success in my businesses in Africa was able to do even more in Europe and elsewhere!

Wherever you are, the key is that God becomes your fortress and that He remains the center of your life. I have seen Him at work from the first day of my conversion in 1981 to this day. My list of testimonies is almost endless, His fidelity lasts forever, my love for Him is limitless, and there is no word to describe Him. We see in **1 Corinthians 12:28** that,

> *"...God has placed in the church first of all apostles, second prophets, third teachers, then miracles, then gifts of*

> ***healing, of helping, of guidance, and of
> different kinds of tongues.***"

For those of you who have a big heart and feel always led to help others, may you be blessed and remain at your post. **It is a calling from God**, so do it with a good heart, humility and enthusiasm.

However, two of the gifts listed above particularly deserve to be emphasized here: "help" (rescue) and "guidance" (administration). Those of you who have the call for governance or administration must do your job with fear and tremble before your God. Not everybody may notice what you are doing and perhaps the people who benefit from your gift don't show any gratefulness. It's just the way it is, people are often blind or ungrateful, and you have to accept it. But God has eyes to see and a hand to reward you at the appointed time. Everything you do, do it with **good conscience and love.**

After I arrived in Europe in 1989, I invested the fruits of the sale of my business into real estate, thus tripling my capital through the expansion I had made there. This move provided me with generated revenues and facilitated the acquisition of other properties in Europe, Africa and the United States.

You may be wondering how this is possible. It is possible because God gives us His children the intelligence to multiply, even when we start from scratch. That is why I wanted to show you that **the management and multiplication of talents is most and foremost a spiritual matter.**

All it takes is an act of obedience to the voice of God. When you are convinced that God is asking you to do something, obey even when you do not understand how you will be able to do it. Obey and He will activate all the gearwheel of that mechanism that will lead you to the success of your business. In the end, *we* are the beneficiaries and consumers of the blessings produced by our obedience.

CHAPTER FIFTEEN

DREAMS, AMBITIONS AND PROJECTS

My dear readers, **I encourage you to believe in yourselves**. Whatever your weakness is, believe in yourself. The world judges you, society despises you, family underestimates you, the Church discourages you, your friends demean you and you look down on yourself! If you are in this situation, I say to you: START BELIEVING IN YOURSELF NOW!

This is a key, if not *the* key you need in order to manifest your full potentials as a person. Again, I know what I am talking about and I was set free from low self-confidence. For years, I lived in a horrible inferiority complex. I thought I was good for nothing, without intelligence, incapable and talentless. I even found myself looking ugly.

Yet everyone had the exact opposite image of me. They thought I was capable, dynamic, with exceptional composure, kind, intelligent and pretty, which leads me to say that what matters is not what others see and think of you, but what *you* see and think of yourself. I don't know where this complex and the sickly shyness I grew up with came from, especially considering the many extraordinary things I had been able to accomplish.

I open my life and heart to you here with the sole purpose of freeing you from that spirit, in the name of Jesus. It is a spiritual matter. The devil is a liar. Get up and walk with your head held high. Your posture, the way you walk, the way you talk, say a lot about your inner state, and be aware of it.

Prayer

Lord, I pray for every person who reads this book that You may free them from all forms of self-deprecation in the name of Jesus.

Holy Spirit of God, please intervene on their behalf so that they may be free from any false accusation from Satan against their lives, in the name of Jesus.

May they be free from the lack of self-esteem, in the name of Jesus.

I release them to you Holy Ghost so that You may walk with them and make them live

*the happiness that is rightfully theirs if they
have self-esteem and believe in themselves.*

*Thank you Lord because I know You've
heard this prayer. Amen!*

Staying in a mindset where you constantly underestimate yourself or block your ability to explore your potentials is a dangerous place to be. Everything that is not explored remains in a latent state where nothing is produced and where you are incapable of evolving. This inner discomfort inevitably leads to a real and serious blockage. And I thank the Lord for having liberated me from it.

If you don't manage to completely get out of that situation, your dreams, your ambitions, your projects, no matter how big, will be difficult to achieve. If you try to achieve them regardless, the results will be below your expectations. And if you are lucky enough to obtain objectively satisfactory results, you will still be unable to rejoice and will always find a way to diminish your merits.

How Did I Break Free?

I will list everything I had undertaken before my deliverance took place. Despite my success, my complex persisted.

While I was still in primary school, I had the idea to start a personal business project. After school-and I guess after my homework-I was busy preparing and caramelizing peanuts. Then I would go to a place I picked waiting for potential clients. This business allowed me to become the first child to open a bank account without her parents' consent, which seems incredible when I think about it now.

I remember someone even asked me for a credit one day, which I accepted. God is great. We are blessed to bless others. I ran my business like a big investment and I put all my heart and my seriousness into it. The work was done with care and quality. I was punctual, friendly with the clients and managed to keep a place for my studies and my little girl life. Despite my success I stayed humble and nice to others. The money was well managed, one part dedicated to the purchase of my merchandise, another to savings.

Several years ago during a conference I hosted through *Bary's Ministries International*, our Non Profit Organization in Rwanda, I gave this testimony as an encouragement to my street children-which we nicknamed our "princes"-and to all the other young people who had come for the soccer game we organized. None of them wanted to believe me. They said to me, "Could a woman like you sell caramelized peanuts when you were our age? It's impossible; she only says that to encourage us."

This soccer game was part of a competition held at the Kigali Stadium and was made up of girls' and boys' teams, with a cup ceremony at the end. After the awards given by Bary's Ministries International, I took the time to share God's Word with the team. "**Being positive where others are negative.**"

In my teenage years, I was a basketball player in a provincial team. I also played soccer, table tennis and volleyball. I then opened my business in the ready-to-wear industry. Despite all my accomplishments, I was shy and hung up. Despite my conversion and my zeal for Jesus, this anomaly stuck with me.

Tired of this lack of self-confidence, I decided to start my very first 7-day dry fast. I thought at times that I was going to die, but I stood firm and determined to go all the way. Although I was not yet called to the ministry, I was very zealous. During that fast, however, I had the impression that God did not care about my problem at all.

I was saddened to see or imagine that God had no compassion for me in this specific area. Oh, the things that He has to hear from his children sometimes! The fact is He does not need to beat the drums to save, heal, bless and deliver. Do you know why we servants of God like to shout during our preaching? It is because subconsciously we think that by shouting people will be more touched and that it will constitute evidence for anointing or power.

Wrong! That is why some of our ministers go so far as to imitate other preachers, renowned for their power, in their mimicry, voice or body language. Sometimes such ministers come to use the same type of towel to wipe their foreheads during their frantic sermons.

A man or woman truly called by God does not need to prove anything. Their role is to seek the face of God in order to cultivate their personal relationship with God. And the anointing will be granted to them for the edification of the body of Christ through the grace that the Holy Ghost will give them according to His will. Therefore the spirit of competition and jealousy in our circles doesn't make sense whatsoever if it is God that we serve truthfully.

It is becoming more and more difficult to distinguish whom we truly serve: God or ourselves. He is not blind and probes every living being. Remember that biblical passage where God speaks to Elijah in **1 Kings 19:11-12:**

> *"The LORD said, "Go out and stand on the mountain in the presence of the LORD, for the LORD is about to pass by.*

> **Then a great and powerful wind tore the mountains apart and shattered the rocks before the LORD, but the LORD was not in the wind. After the wind there was an earthquake, but the LORD was not in the earthquake.**
>
> **[12] After the earthquake came a fire, but the LORD was not in the fire. And after the fire came a gentle whisper."**

During my dry fast, at no time did I feel that I was having a good time spiritually, nor that what I was doing was approved by God. The whole thing felt completely empty. I would like to encourage you by saying that every spiritual process you start makes sense and hides results that will come out eventually.

So I ended this period of abstinence on a sad note, having felt nothing tangible spiritually, but I was nevertheless pleased to have resisted for seven days to the temptation to cheat or eat. Years passed before I finally realized that my deliverance had been granted since that day!

Liberation

The Eternal God, despite His silence, had thus approved my fast and time of prayer! However, I'm not telling you to do exactly like I did to reach your solution. I just wanted to share my journey with you. The moment you break free, your dreams and ambitions are released, your projects come true, your mind becomes flexible, determined and full of confidence.

Even when you run into trouble, be optimistic and carry on. Life is not just about getting married, having children, getting a job, building a career, buying a house, a car or starting a ministry. You have to be fulfilled through what you are passionate about, your projects, your dreams putting Christ at the center of it all. Here is a song that comes to my mind:

The Eternal God is in your midst
Like a hero who saves
He will make you His greatest joy
You'll remain silent in His presence
You'll tremble with cries of joy

The purpose of this book is for you to break free from your chains. And I know it will happen in the name of Jesus.

CHAPTER SIXTEEN

HAVE NO REGRETS

Life is made of successive stages that have their own importance and specificity. Just like in meteorology where there are seasons, low and high pressures, our personal lives go through seasons punctuated by "ups and downs".

There are seasons where every little thing goes perfectly well according to the plan, where you are satisfied, where you succeed in everything you do, and where you feel like you accomplish your goals. People think you are great, they welcome you, and they seek your friendship and praise you. They talk about you as a reference, the flatteries, the smiles and winks become the norm for you. They pat you on the back, give you hugs and invite you to the most prestigious places. Text messages and phone calls never seem to stop either.

In short, you are on cloud nine. It is as if there was a supernatural strength and ability in you, an indescribable happiness and joy. You smile, you whistle, your eyes flicker. This is what I call the **high season**, a watered and flowered time of your life.

Then there's this other, gloomier season. It usually offers a state of severe depression. Some spiritually immature people even claim that true Christians should never find themselves in depression. Nothing could be further from the truth! Read the statistics on the subject, they are very telling. Indeed, you will find that many servants of God and ministers also go through depression. That is why many have abandoned their ministry or calling. It's truly traumatic. If you are reading this and find yourself in this situation, I urge you to take up your torch, lift up your banner and walk again to accomplish what God created and called you for.

The **low season** can be very easily defined: "This is the end of the line", "Abandon the ship, now!" It is a period of stagnation, decline and regression. None of your projects work, success eludes you, despite your good will, your efforts, and your investment of time, energy and money. All doors are closed. No one considers or appreciates you. It is even difficult to have any support from your friends, family and acquaintances. You're being singled out, people are talking behind your back, and they're running away from you. The phone is silent, not one call, not even from the brothers and sisters of your congregation.

During this season, you no longer have the right to speak because your opinion is considered worthless, and your spiritual gifts are no more recognized. Some will even tell you "Use your spiritual gifts for your own benefit before helping others", or using the biblical reference "**Physician heal thyself**" (Luke 4:23). Always have in mind that the people who saw Jesus crucified had exactly the same attitude, as we can read in **Luke 23:35-37**,

> *"The people stood watching, and the rulers even sneered at him. They said, "He saved others; let him save himself if he is God's Messiah, the Chosen One."*
>
> *The soldiers also came up and mocked him. They offered him wine vinegar and said, "If you are the king of the Jews, save yourself."*

In this low season, even the people you have done good to will look down on you, forgetting how you blessed them in their own low season. Don't be surprised if you are given "funny" nicknames. Doesn't the Bible say that, *"Man's heart is tortuous and wicked."* If you still live in a world similar to the one of "My Little Pony", I beg you to wake up quickly before you end up swallowed and crushed by the very people you would never suspect to hurt you.

However, having this kind of mindset doesn't necessarily mean being suspicious of everything and everybody. This is called having wisdom. In any case, woe to you who curse, reject and despise those who find themselves in their low season! Isn't it true that the Bible says,

> *"Do not be deceived: God cannot be mocked. A man reaps what he sows."* **(Galatians 6:7)?**

> *"Whoever digs a pit will fall there; if someone rolls a stone, it will roll back to them."* **(Proverbs 26:27)?**

> *"He who stirs stones will be hurt, and he who splits wood will be in danger."* **(Ecclesiastes 10:9)?**

Dear readers, I urge you to always have a heart to do good, to speak well about others, to defend and support every person who find themselves in difficulties, to think positively of people and to help others.

But at the risk of throwing you off balance here, let me also tell you this: it is a real mistake to consider the low season as a bad thing. On the contrary, this period is a real opportunity to make us solid, stable, determined, patient, persevering, firm and mature. It is in that period that we discern the true identity of the people around us. There we discover:

- who is faithful and loyal to us
- who believes in us despite rejection and contempt
- who defends us when we are insulted, criticized, slandered and falsely accused
- who will be able to support our arms as we raise them to heaven in the battle, like Aaron and Moses did
- Who will tell us, "You're going to be fine, the storm will be over soon!"

This low season aims to work and shape who we are according to the blueprint of the "Good Potter". A season where we are clay in His hands, where the trials we pass through are a perfect platform for our emotional, spiritual, physical, moral and sentimental "retouching".

CHAPTER SEVENTEEN

OVERCOMING THE VANITY OF LIFE

Let us consider for a moment the book of the Ecclesiastes written in the 10th Century BC, its author Solomon is described by the Hebrew term "*Koheleth*", implying that he is both a teacher/preacher and the king of Israel in Jerusalem.

For Solomon, the term "vanity" refers to something that is empty, with no permanent value and that leads to a feeling of dissatisfaction. In analyzing the first verses of the first chapter, he states that it is indeed a vanity to be born, to struggle, to suffer or to experience temporary joys that have nothing to do with eternity. Then one will eventually have to leave everything behind and die.

To paraphrase King Solomon: what exactly are we looking for in life? Let's think about it for a moment because you'll see that giving a clear answer is not an easy task. The Bible states that,

"In vain you rise early and stay up late, toiling for food to eat— for he grants sleep to those He loves."

Ecclesiastes 2:22 *"What do people get for all the toil and anxious striving with which they labor under the sun?"*

Verse 23 of the same chapter speaks of pain, sorrow, and our heart finds no rest at night. If you too can't find sleep at night while you lie in bed, this verse is about you. Your mind is active because of the problems and hassles that come up from your heart. Be free today in the name of Jesus!

What every man and woman is really looking for is simple: happiness and rest. Solomon concludes after all his experiences by saying, *"Fear God, keep His commandments."*

The Importance of Knowing your Direction

It's easier to continue your journey when you know where you're going. Having a direction provides confidence despite the wanderings, trials and errors that will occur here and there on the way. It will lead you to the right paths and make you use the appropriate means to reach your final destination.

You will have peace regardless of the difficulties and oppositions. Where to turn to find the help we need? Up or down, before or behind us, right or left? Nature can sometimes provide us with answers. Indeed, even plants look up to the sky to maximize their exposure to the sunrays or the raindrops, and thus their ability to develop more gracefully and beautifully. The same goes for animals: they lift up their head when they call for help. If you cry, weep lifting your head to heaven, to the Eternal God!

Let's take the example of Hannah, mother of the Prophet Samuel, and Sarah, mother of Isaac. Both directed their tears upwards and produced two giants in the faith. Crying downwards or turning backwards will lead you to abandonment and frustration. Looking up is always the best option.

In **1 Samuel 1:1-28**, we read that Hannah's husband Elkanah went up to Shiloh. This ascent had several consequences: an encounter with Eli, spoken words of blessing about his wife, Samuel's birth and Samuel's service to God.

In **Genesis 28:12**, Jacob had the vision of a ladder *"resting on the earth, with its top reaching to heaven, and the angels of God were ascending and descending on it."*

This encounter was a vision from God. This vision revealed God's promise to him to give him and his seed the land, and that in his seed shall all the families of the earth shall be blessed. Beyond that, God promised to keep him in all his ways and also bring him back to the land. God concluded, saying-".. *I will not leave thee, until I have done that which I have spoken to thee of.*" (Genesis 28:13-15).

Jacob woke up from sleep terribly shaken. He was afraid, and declared the place a dreadful one, the house of God and the gate of heaven. He set up the stone he used as pillows, raised it as an altar, poured oil on it and called the place Bethel (meaning the house of God) *"And Jacob vowed a vow, saying, If God will be with me, and will keep me in this way that I go, and will give me bread to eat, and raiment to put on, So that I come again to my father's house in peace; then shall the LORD be my God: And this stone, which I have set for a pillar, shall be God's house: and of all that thou shalt give me I will surely give the tenth unto thee.*" (Genesis 28:20-22).

In response to God's promise to keep him in all his ways, Jacob vowed that if God gave him food and clothing as I return alive to my father's house in peace, the Lord shall be my God, this place shall become God's house and I shall give the tenth (tithe) of all you gave me. He understood the principle of appreciating God with giving God his own portion. This principle when observed is loaded with covenant blessings as we read in **Malachi 3:10-12**:

> *"'Bring the whole tithe into the storehouse, that there may be food in my house. Test me in this,' says the LORD Almighty, 'and see if I will not throw open the floodgates of heaven and pour out so much blessing that there will not be room enough to store it.*
>
> *I will prevent pests from devouring your crops, and the vines in your fields will not drop their fruit before it is ripe,' says the LORD Almighty.*
>
> *Then all the nations will call you blessed, for yours will be a delightful land,' says the LORD Almighty."*

The encounter of Jacob and his response to God is a revelation of a man on a journey with God, and that is the kind of man God uses. He looked up, saw God and connected with God's divine plan and move on his life. As we encounter God we must look, lift up our eyes unto the Lord, our maker and helper.

From this vision, many things flowed into Jacob's life: the meeting with Rachel, the descendants born from their union (Joseph and Benjamin) and the reconciliation with his brother Esau. Strength, courage, energy, youth, vision, knowledge, patience and perseverance are traits that come to us from above. So, look up unto the Lord!

Inversely, looking downwards can bring depression, unproductiveness and fatigue. Typically, the lazy, weak-minded, visionless, ambitionless, coward, timid and irresolute individuals will look in that direction. When you do all you see is discouragement, despair, limitations, frustrations, disappointments and failures in life.

My question to you now is "What is your place in your family, your society, your church?" If you've found it, learn to grow in it and be productive where you are. It's for this reason that the Father cuts us back, prunes us and replants us as needed (John 15). Pruning is performed through the circumstances of life and trials. After that period of cutting and breaking come development, growth and happiness. It's a time when you can reap. God bless you.

Remember ye not the former things,
Neither consider the things of old.
Behold, I will do a new thing; now it
Shall spring forth; shall ye not know it?

-Isaiah 43: 18-19

Delight thyself also in the LORD;
and he shall give thee the desires of thine heart.
-Proverbs 34:4

COMING SOON

1. Rebuild on The Ruins, It's Possible.
2. French Cuisine Education.
3. The Consequences of Alcoholism Addiction
4. The Benefits of Fast and Prayer

To Buy Book in Belgium

Baributsa & Pierlot Consulting (B&P-C)

Tel: 003-2471-601-680

Email: Pierlot.roland@gmail.com

Editing and Publishing by:

Baributsa & Pierlot Consulting (B&P-C)

Phone: 214-470-2189

Email: barysministries@yahoo.fr

Fb: Apostle Melody Jacqueline

www.Baributsa&Pierlot.com

Bary's Ministries Street Boys in their Center in Kigali having a Bible Study after school, March 2005.

Completion of Bary's Ministries Social Center in Nyamata where actually widow are trained.

Mission in Goma East Congo/DRC to the Street's Boys.

Mission in Kenya in Meru near (Mount Kenya).
Praying for students from different Universities.
She taught about "The Power of The Holy Spirit"

Girls' team after the football match she organize
on Nyamirambo Stadium in Kigali/Rwanda.

Inauguration and Dedication of her Land
in Nyamata/Rwanda in 2005.

Bary's Boys at school doing Auto-
Mechanic Training at JOC in Kigali.

Bary's Ministries Street Boys working in their
garden planting vegetables, in Kigali.

Mission in Gisenyi/Rwanda. One of these people became members of Barry's Ministries 12 years later here in America.

Printed in the United States
By Bookmasters